You must get up at dawn to fish for lobsters.

3

Pull on boots and warm clothes.
It can be cold on the water all year round.

4

You can help carry this basket of raw fish.
We'll use it for bait.

Now I'll haul in the anchor.

We'll head for the rocks.
That's where lobsters like to crawl
around under the salt water.

Look for a small marker like this.

Each person has a different color.

Our color is blue.

There's a blue marker!
We'll grab it with this hook.
The hook is called a gaff.

9

Now we have to haul up the rope.

The trap is down there under the salt water.

Pull hard. The trap is heavy.

10

Look! We caught two lobsters.
Watch out for those claws.

This lobster is too small.
We'll throw it back so it can grow.

Now put some more raw fish on the hook.

Lobsters will crawl into the trap to get the bait.

But they can't crawl back out.

13

On to the next trap!
We'll haul about a hundred traps today.

14

Look at all the lobsters we caught.

Now it's time to call home.

We're coming in.

Lobster Fishing
at Dawn

Written by Robert Newell
Photographed by Paul Dyer